Ling,
the Star Painter

Written and illustrated by Sue Cheung

Collins

Yan is painting flowers in the garden, but his sister, Ling, is marching and tooting her trumpet.

"Stop that racket," Yan complains.
"But I am a star!" Ling exclaims.
"Stand by that tree," says Yan.
"Then you can screech as much
as you like."

3

Ling scoots off and stoops to pick up a trowel. She taps the trowel on a tree trunk. Click, clack!

She scoops up grains of sand.
Crunch, crunch! Then she drums
the steel dustbin. Bang, thump!

Yan frowns. "That is too much clattering!" he yells.

"But I am a star!" blurts Ling.

Yan is stern. "You will be a bigger star if you stop bothering me," he says.

Ling gets the point. So she pushes
the bamboo with the trowel.
Swish, swish.

She squelches in the mud.

Then ... she steps onto three planks of wood. Snap, crash, bang!

"Ow!" Ling yells, rubbing her hurt leg.

Ling sees a snail and steps across it to avoid squishing it, but her right sock snags on a rock.

Ling trips on a broom and lands on the paint. Green and scarlet spurt out.

"My painting is spoiled!" groans Yan.
He looks disappointed at the smear.
But then it is clear. The blooms do not
look boring now ...

They are bright and elegant!
"You are a star!" says Yan.
"A star painter!"

Ling and Yan

🐾 Review: After reading 🐾

Use your assessment from hearing the children read to choose any GPCs, words or tricky words that need additional practice.

Read 1: Decoding

- Turn to pages 4 and 5 and look for words with long vowels and adjacent consonants. Model sounding out **s/c/oo/t/s**. Point to the following and ask the children to sound them out: **stoops**, **tree**, **scoops**, **grains**, **steel**.

- Ask the children to sound out longer words, breaking them into chunks or syllables to help, if necessary.

  ex/claims   **scar/let**   **dis/a/ppoint/ed**   **paint/ing**

- On page 6, ask children to read some of Yan's spoken words aloud. Say: Can you blend in your head when you read these words?

Read 2: Prosody

- Read pages 6 and 7 expressively, using different voices for Yan and Ling, and emphasising the sound words.

- Ask children to work in pairs to practise reading the pages to each other like a storyteller, making the story sound as fun and exciting as they can.

- Encourage the children to offer positive feedback to each other. Prompt by asking: Can you make Yan sound even more annoyed? Can you make the sound words funnier by exaggerating their sounds?

Read 3: Comprehension

- Ask the children if they've ever been disturbed by noise – what was it? What happened?

- Discuss the meaning of the phrases **scoots off** (page 4) and **gets the point** (page 7). Ask the children to read the text and explain the meaning. Ask: Can you explain what Ling does in your own words? (e.g. *runs off, understands she has to be quiet*)

- Turn to page 6 and point to **star**. Ask: Why did Ling make so much noise? What sort of star did she want to be? (e.g. *she was practising making music, or playing drums; she wanted to be a star in a music band*)

- Look together at pages 14 and 15. Encourage the children to use the pictures to help them retell the story in the correct sequence.